Keeping the Public in Public Education

© 2012, Rick Salutin
All rights reserved. No part of this book may be reproduced, for any reason, by any means, without the permission of the publisher.

Cover design by Debbie Geltner.
Photo of Author by Marketa Russell Holtebrinck.

Many thanks to:
At the Toronto Star: Alison Uncles, Joe Hall, Glen Colbourn, Andrew Phillips, John Cruickshank and John Honderich;
At the Atkinson Foundation: Charles Pascal and Elizabeth Chan;
In Finland: everyone I met but especially Pasi Sahlberg, Peter Johnson and Marja Alopaeus;
In Saskatchewan: everyone I met but especially Michael Tymchak and Mike LeClaire.
And everyone else I talked with but especially the following: Carolyn Acker, David Booth, Luther Brown, Donald Eckler, Christa Freiler, Grace-Edward Galabuzi, Alana Grossman, Lisa Guthro, Wendy Hughes, Annie Kidder, Ben Levin, Hugh Mackenzie, Kathleen Gallagher, Penny Milton, Duszan Petrocic, Mari Rutka, Barrie Sketchley, Chris Spence, Nancy Steinhauer, Gay Stephenson, Charles Ungerleider and Sue Winton.

Printed and bound in Canada by Marquis Book Printing Inc.

Library and Archives Canada Cataloguing in Publication

Salutin, Rick, 1942-
    Keeping the public in public education / Rick Salutin.

Also issued in electronic format.
ISBN 978-0-9878317-2-9

    1. Public schools--Social aspects. 2. Education--Social aspects.
3. Public schools--Social aspects--Canada. 4. Education--Social aspects--Canada. I. Title.

LC191.S24 2012   370   C2011-907677-2

SINGLES
Linda Leith Publishing Inc.
www.lindaleith.com

.ll.

Keeping the Public in Public Education

RICK SALUTIN

LINDA LEITH
PUBLISHING

*For Mrs. McCuaig,
Mr. Colgrove
and all the other teachers*

Contents

Introduction: The Sector That Dares Not Speak Its Name 7

   I. The Teaching Piece 19

   II. Against Choice 28

   III. Testing, testing ... You're fired! 38

   IV. Equity: Who Are "We" Now? 48

   V. What is Public about Public Education? 56

Introduction: The Sector That Dares Not Speak Its Name

These are strange times. The private sector, whatever that means exactly, seems able to do no wrong — and to shake off any wrong it does — while the public sector dares not utter its name for fear of derision and worse.

For 30 to 40 years, everywhere in the world, the private sector has proceeded from triumph to triumph. It shook off or loosened most of the regulations that were imposed on it after the Great Depression and the economic disaster of the 1930s. Those included limits on expansion and monopoly that were meant, in the spirit of capitalism's own creed, to guarantee the benefits of competition. Rules were laid down to prevent fraud and deception, along with subtler forms of manipulation.

Many of those controls have now been eliminated. Where they persist, the bodies charged with investigating and applying them have been starved for funding and staff. A revolving door exists through which regulators and the regulated change places — regularly. This leaves the oversight bodies with little reason to act seriously, not to mention severely, with their prospective employers.

The same is true of regulation in other areas, like the environment. The New York Times reported in September of 2011, "an ExxonMobil pipeline carrying oil across Montana burst suddenly, soiling the swollen Yellowstone River with an estimated 42,000 gallons of crude just weeks after a company inspection and federal review had found nothing seriously wrong." The story was headed, "Pipeline agency chronically undermanned."

In Canada under the Harper government, the current round of deregulation combined with undermining oversight meant getting rid of the President of the Canadian Wheat Board, the Chair of the Nuclear Safety Commission, and, by way of his resignation after a bitter conflict over the census, the head of Statistics Canada. The ability to assemble data in order to figure out what's going wrong in the country has been undercut by eliminating the long form of the national census along with a database that had been used for access-to-information requests.

A major constraint on reckless behaviour by employers – collective activity by their employees in the form of trade unionism – was attacked and weakened. The opening shots were fired by President Ronald Reagan against air traffic controllers in the U.S. in 1981 and by Prime Minister Margaret Thatcher against miners in the U.K. in 1984-85. Companies spent freely to develop strategies and train management in techniques for combating and intimidating unions. Anti-union experts and consultants flourished.

This was accompanied by a parallel cultural assault. The labour beat disappeared in the news media, while business coverage expanded massively, including pro-business programming on public broadcasters like PBS in the U.S. and CBC in Canada. In 2011, CBC promoted its nightly hour on business on television in the words of host-journalist Amanda Lang: "I think what is really special about the show is that it does celebrate business." No one in the world of media was celebrating labour or the public sector – and definitely not for an hour each night. Union membership declined severely. Even where contracts still existed, employers increasingly violated them, knowing there was little chance of enforcement by governmental labour boards. One sign of victory in this contest: the gap between CEOs and their employees rose to 325 times what the latter earned. Fifty years earlier, it had been about 25-1.

In North America, part of this triumphal advance was a strategy to generate higher profits by using agreements on free trade to move production to areas of cheaper labour. So Canadian factories shut down; their equipment and jobs were shipped, often in the first instance to southern U.S. states, many of which had anti-labour laws, or from the U.S. to Mexico. Then, if labour in those places became too costly, the jobs moved again, sometimes to China, and on from there when costs rose again.

This left a problem: how to continue making good money in the (formerly) home markets, where workers' wages and purchasing power had stagnated or fallen. Part of the answer was to siphon off some of the money that seemed to be sloshing around in the public sector, in areas like health care and education, funded by taxes. In the U.S., although the medical sector was largely private, there were substantial public expenditures on the elderly and the poor. Large corporations in the form of Health Management Organizations (HMOs) moved in on funding sources that had been previously dominated by individual GPs and specialists, while during the George W. Bush years drug companies successfully lobbied for laws that gave them privileged access to the same public money.

In Canada and the U.K., soothing names like public-private partnerships were used in the construction of new hospitals and highways: the bulk of money spent and the risks taken were public but the profits were private. Public education was harder to exploit but offered a huge pool of potential profit; it was tapped, for example, by way of vouchers used to pay for private schooling with public funds, indirect privatization via "charter" schools, again paid for publicly, or by establishing highly profitable standardized testing and marketing businesses, consulting firms, etc.

The economic collapse of 2008 (and counting), in which millions lost jobs and homes, centered on the financial sector. Its roots were planted a decade earlier, during the "liberal" Clinton era in the U.S. and the New Labour Blair era in the U.K., through deregulation of financial markets and institutions. That led to "self-dealing," by which banks and others were free to rig and hide dubious transactions done with new devices they invented that were incomprehensible. These contraptions had impenetrable names like credit default swaps and bundled mortgages. They cleared the way for the housing bubble in the U.S., which spread its effects everywhere owing to the globalization of financial markets.

Behind the housing bubble was a desperate need for expansion of consumer credit in the U.S. in order to sustain growth in its economy – and that of the rest of the world, which had grown dependent on exporting products to the U.S. With the decline of wages among average Americans, consumer demand in the U.S. had dwindled over the years of free trade and job export. Americans' overvalued homes became their private ATMs, until the bubble burst.

When that happened, with impacts everywhere, and financial institutions like Lehman Brothers began to implode, the private sector summoned the public sector to its aid. It came swiftly, even in the midst of a U.S. presidential election. Huge bailouts followed, paid for with the tax money of ordinary citizens, and those financial institutions which now dominated the private sector in the U.S. survived, or at worst were taken over (with the exception of Lehman Brothers, R.I.P.). The carnage among homeowners and ordinary working people was vast. At no point did the financial institutions, bankers or the diminishing number of captains of industry admit any serious responsibility. They never waived their huge incomes or bonuses. They continued to pay and over-reward themselves, even as joblessness and home foreclosures rose. That refusal to accept responsibility was even more offensive than the greed. Who knows where it might eventually lead? There was no serious re-regulation to assure it all wouldn't happen again, and soon. The revolving door continued to spin. The recovery was tepid. At the moment another, deeper, crash seems imminent.

This time though, a few short years later, the solution generally proposed appears to be not another bailout of the private sector by the public, but an attack on the public sector itself, as if it created the mess to start with. This is what is so peculiar about our times. Governments that shouldered large debts in order to bail out the wild partiers of the financial world have now turned on their own citizens and demanded sacrifices – in the form of cuts to services like health care, schools, police and fire protection, or infrastructure such as roads, bridges and sewers – to pay for the bailouts of the past, as if any of that cutting will prevent the unfolding disasters in the present. There is little or no argument made for this response; it seems to be taken for granted by decision-makers. At most they mouth phrases about encouraging the job-creators – i.e., the very business people who created the debacle, and who have not lacked encouragement for four decades at least. Mitt Romney, an ostensible moderate running for U.S. president, says. "The only thing that's stopping us is government and we're gonna say let's stop government and get going again."

There is a religious mentality at work here in this sense: it is based on faith, not facts. Because it is based on faith, it cannot be shaken by anything that actually happens in the world of facts. Since the private sector is inherently good (or sacred) and the public sector is inherently evil (or unholy), whatever ill occurs in the economy must be a result of the public component; its very existence reveals our lack of faith – i.e., faith in the private sector.

The sign that we are cursed is that our lives are hard and worsening. We have not been faithful enough to the tenets of our belief system. None of the pain and debacle is a result of zealously unleashing an irresponsible private sector; it is the result of not unleashing it enough. It is not the consequence of having too little public oversight and counterweight; it is the result of still having too much. It is inevitably, even if invisibly, due to our lack of faith.

This is common in the history of religion. When messianic movements fail, along with the messiahs themselves, the legions of believers tend to blame their own absence of faith. When Jesus of Nazareth was crucified by the Romans, his followers doubled down on their belief: he was gone only until the world was truly ready for his return and the salvation he would bring. Then followed two thousand plus years of preparation. True believers are not easily discouraged. His return has been expected many times since, including 2010 and 2012.

It is unlikely there will be a falloff in expectation after he again fails to show. When the Jewish messiah of the 17th century, Shabtai Zvi, converted to Islam under threat of impalement by the Turkish sultan, his followers found a reason: he had gone underground in the royal court to secretly seek out and destroy the forces of evil that prevented him from fulfilling his promise to lead his people back to their land and restore the primal wholeness of the cosmos. "Turning Turk" was a strategy, proving their faith in him had been right and true all along.

So, in terms of the assault on the public sector that occurred over the past decades, it simply wasn't vigorous enough. The fervour was too restrained. More austerity on the public side is required. Tighten the tourniquet until almost nothing gets through. Starve government and starve the institutions through which it provides the public with essential services it cannot provide for itself, like highways, airports, hospitals and schools. And then allow the private sector to provide these, even though all evidence shows that the private sector does it no better and usually worse, while pocketing the profits. It's a matter of faith.

That faith spreads through the public sector itself; no one is immune. Canny deputy ministers of the pre-Mulroney era in Canada quickly picked up the new message during the 1980s. "Our job now is to dismantle everything we built up in the previous decades," one of them told another, who hadn't yet quite caught the drift. Those high-level civil servants were often among the best and brightest; they were ambitious, and they wanted satisfying, influential, well-paid careers. It often didn't matter to them whether those careers were in the public or the private sector. (That's the case for most, though not all; some were genuinely committed to what the public sector represented. Think former chief of staff to the prime minister and ambassador to the U.S., Derek Burney – who made the switch to big-time CEO in the private sector – versus lifelong civil servant and academic Bernard Ostry, who didn't.)

You can include politicians in this generalization. They all want to win elections, but those most in tune with the times now want to govern in order to dilute, diminish or even destroy government. They say this proudly and apparently sincerely, though it's hard to know what sense it makes. I've never fully understood why people like Preston Manning and Stephen Harper want to become one of the governments they so dislike.

John Lanchester noted in the *London Review of Books* that the European country that has done best in the latest crisis is Belgium, which has no government due to a political stalemate. This has led to a sort of automatic extension of the normal public expenditures that were previously in place. Meanwhile there is no anti-government Belgian government to implement all the cuts and austerity measures recently established by other nations. The result has been healthy growth there compared to the rest of Europe. "It turns out," wrote Lanchester, "that from the economic point of view, in the current crisis, no government is better than any government – any existing government."

Ah yes: in tune with the times. There is a Zeitgeist, a spirit or temper of the age. You feel it in the tones of those with access to public platforms and loudspeakers. Even the people considered, or maligned as, left wing defend the public sector these days only with great caution, severe limitations and many qualifications; without real, or at any rate without clearly expressed, conviction.

They focus narrowly, perhaps on the relatively uncontroversial realm of "infrastructure," which doesn't get ideological pulses racing, like health care or education. Especially when it refers to small-scale projects like local roads, bridges or sewers, fallen into decay, where the private sector hasn't yet figured out how to make huge profits from them, as it has in health care and schools. Even then they speak delicately and defensively about restoring some of those facilities.

Those who are more marginal to the political process can sometimes afford to be slightly more affirmative. So the designer of New York City's High Line project, which created a large new area of park space where an abandoned rail line once stood, was willing to say: "For the longest time, public space has been treated very shabbily, people act like it's just going to be used by the homeless or be subject to disrepair. Now people see that well-designed public space can be a huge asset and transform the culture and the quality of life in a city."

The Zeitgeist, however – sometimes cleverly garbed as "public opinion" – is never quite what it seems. It isn't what "everybody" actually thinks; it's more like what everybody thinks they should think, or thinks everybody else thinks they should think, or what no one better say out loud. In reality it has a lot to do with what those who have control over the main issues in a society prefer to have discussed: what is permissible to say about those issues and how to frame them; what's allowed into the debate versus what will never get mentioned in polite, respectable company: the stuff that would make you feel you just farted or belched if you said it aloud. There is in fact a kind of mass schizophrenia in the actual lived world of "the public," where opinions are far more diverse and oppositional than you'd expect from monitoring the usual reliable sources.

There is a body of polling, for instance, that suggests strong public support for substantially increased taxation of the rich; it never finds expression in the policy debates. Even in the U.S., there has for many decades been a substantial majority, about two-thirds, in favour of a "Canadian-style" single payer health care system. That's nothing you'd suspect from the way the issue has been presented throughout that period. But the schizophrenia involved runs deep; and if pressed about health care, the same people might shy away or pull back from that support, knowing it's out of step. Besides, when the issue was actually presented for debate in concrete legislative form by the Obama government in 2009, many of those same people opposed the very mild and "sub-Canadian" version of universal health care he presented, perhaps because they were frightened off by tales of "death panels" and other scare tactics – or in some cases possibly because it wasn't "Canadian" enough.

I'm not saying the issue of public opinion is a simple one. But even on the subject of capitalism or, as it's usually called, the free market, "there has been a sharp fall in the number of Americans who think that the free market economy is the best economic system for the future." "Support," says Globespan, an 'international opinion research consultancy' which seems as respectable as most, "has plummeted since 2009, falling 15 points in a year so that fewer than three in five (59 percent) now see free market capitalism as the best system for the future."

What do we really know, for that matter, about "public opinion" even during the great epochs of religious faith in the past? We're dependent on the written sources, dominated by the people who could write, who were, or were beholden to, the religious and secular authorities. How many ordinary folk listened uncritically in the pews as the priest explained, every Sunday (or every Friday in the Muslim world) why everything was for the best in the order of things as it existed. How many rolled their eyes or smiled wryly at each other? We just don't know. The same applies to the cheering masses in the streets as the new king or leader passed to or from a coronation or inauguration.

The conflict between public and private has been muted in recent decades, which was not the case for much of the 20th century. In the U.S., the only realm that is defiantly public and proud isn't usually thought of as public in the public sector sense at all: the American military. Economist Milton Friedman, the patron saint of unrestricted free market economics, said he strove all his life to find a way to privatize the armed forces because it was such an exception to the capitalist system he idealized and promoted – but he failed. Nevertheless, the U.S. military has, since the Second World War, largely functioned as a make-work, or make-profit, project for the private sector. It's hard to imagine how American capitalism would look without the huge boost it has received from military spending and research. Many of the innovations that powered the U.S. economy, including the computer and the Internet, originated in public spending by the Department of Defense, the results of which were transferred virtually without cost to private corporations, who certainly knew how to exploit them.

In the U.K., the public sector has existed most prominently in the form of the National Health Service, which is one of Britain's proudest achievements. It has issues, like every huge institution, but no serious frontal attack has ever been launched against it. It has been seriously undermined, during these decades of private sector triumphalism, but only by stealth. The Labour government of Tony Blair initiated numerous "reforms" that amounted to steps towards privatization. They often used language implying the opposite and always denied that privatization was their intent. It was all justified in the name of efficiency and better service.

Now, under the Conservative-led coalition government, a full-scale version of privatization without nearly so much subterfuge is taking place. What still hasn't had a serious airing, though it may receive one in the political light of day, is the question of the differences between a genuinely public health care system and one that is largely private but run with mostly public money. That difference has to do with one system – public – in which the explicit aims are patient welfare, versus another system – the private one – which necessarily focuses on corporate profits, and that claims to maximize patient welfare precisely because it concentrates on making money rather than on human health. This kind of argument displays capitalism at its most robust and paradoxical. If that debate ever occurs it would be invigorating and politically healthy. It would be far preferable to the sneaky creep of privatization.

For reasons not very clear to me, the Canadian system of universal health care has so far survived reasonably well. It has been criticized and pronounced unsustainable by the same sources as elsewhere: private think tanks, medical corporations, columnists, experts, consultants, and all political parties. You could say the only people in favour of leaving the Canadian system in place have been the people themselves (with rare exceptions like Roy Romanow, in his report during the Jean Chretien years). Yet it has survived because so far Canadians have been unwilling to buy into the arguments that what we have is simply impossible to maintain. Their ability to maintain skepticism in the face of endless authoritative rebukes and reprimands has been inspiring.

What follows is an effort to explore this conflict in the area of public education. Much of it first appeared as a series in the Toronto Star in the spring of 2011, underwritten by the Atkinson Foundation.

Some time after the series appeared, the dean of a university education faculty told me that many of her colleagues had read the series with a sense of relief at seeing the issues that preoccupied them openly discussed and defended. Evoking a sense of relief is a great reaction to get for a writer. What you're always hoping for is some kindred sense of recognition. The readers feel they have not been alone and the writer feels no longer isolated in his thoughts. You don't want to simply echo what readers already know, but you don't want to prattle on all by yourself either. All learning, Plato said in the Meno, is really recollection. How could we recognize something as true if we didn't already in some way know it – even if we have, somehow, forgotten it? I offer this project in that spirit.

I. The Teaching Piece

In the fall of 2010, I attended a talky, high-powered Toronto education conference well-stocked with big international players. I took a few hours off to see a class in a nearby school. The class was already in session when the vice-principal showed me in and shut the door. I looked around. The kids were rapt. That's when it hit me: You shut the door of the classroom behind you and all bets are off.

The whole range of topics at the conference – curriculum, "effective teaching," leadership – stops when that door shuts. Improvement in achievement comes from good instruction, says former B.C. deputy education minister, Charles Ungerleider, not from anything else. Kids know it. How could they not? They're in there with that teacher five or six hours a day every day in the early years and x number of periods later on. It's like being stuck with your family. It works or it doesn't. Teachers know it and that may be why they often react wearily to the endless trends and fads that wash over their world.

Donald Eckler at Clinton Public School would surely count as a master teacher of Grade 6, and not just based on 35 years in the classroom. "Every few years, teachers have to jump through new hoops," he says:

> Like a few years ago. All classes had to do a DPA, Daily Physical Activity. 30 minutes uninterrupted. It was a big deal, it came from Ontario Premier Dalton McGuinty. There were workshops. But there was nowhere to do it. So teachers end up dragging kids up and down stairs. Do jumping jacks. Then

slowly you realize no one really cares so you stop. Literally nobody was doing it. Like there's a total disconnect from wherever they issue these edicts.

It's the same when HQ announces big changes in report cards. "You do a lot of eye-rolling as you hear the latest hoop to jump through." That's how it looks from the ground up, after you close that door.

I'm instantly tempted to apologize for using an anecdote. Education is an area rife with stats and studies. But what almost anyone recalls from their school years – ask yourself – is a teacher or two. For me it might be Mrs. McCuaig, who wrote in the margin of an essay, beside a smudge, "Food for thought?"

This isn't accidental. It's the essence of the school experience. It's a relationship. It needn't even be a teacher. Ungerleider once studied why potential dropouts did not in fact drop out. One kid stayed because an adult smiled and asked how he was in the hall each day. He didn't know who it was. Turned out to be a janitor. At Clinton it might be Zilda Silva in the office. To kids, she's an anchor. At Grade 6 graduation, she got more valedictory accolades than any teacher. When the key is a living relationship, you don't quantify it. You recount it.

Now ask what you got from that teacher. Was it some info they passed on, or was it something they ignited in you? Probably the latter. Kids don't need to be taught that much; they're natural learners. They learn from birth, prodigiously. Everyone learns to walk and talk, without teachers – far harder tasks than anything to follow. The true mystery is that many kids lose their knack for learning, at least during school hours. That's why ignition is the ticket.

Since it's a relationship, teaching is a living thing that's hard to nail down. It's more a practice than a technique.

And since it's a relationship, almost anything can and does work. That's its most puzzling feature. So much works — because, as a relationship, it's built on the needs of students and the strengths of teachers, which can vary as much as human nature. So the possible ways to teach are endless. It's like therapy, where distinct, even contradictory methods can all get results if there's a strong relationship. Without that, nothing gels.

So, for example, teachers try to teach kids to think. But as American philosopher of education John Dewey said, "There is no method of thinking. Thinking is the method of thinking." How do you teach that? Your way. Donald Eckler uses "mind traps" to get students thinking "laterally." It works for him, because it's how his mind gets ignited. Principal Barrie Sketchley of Rosedale Heights Arts School, who has worked at all levels of the system, says if a teacher stands and talks at the front of the class and does it well, that's fine. A talking head can work.

Consider a crucial area: reading. Wars have been fought over how to teach it: phonics versus whole word versus just being read to, etc. It's so silly. Learning to read recapitulates the whole history of our species, in its momentous transition from the oral to the written tradition starting 6,000 years ago. Have some humility. There's no one right way to do that. You can kill the process if you insist there is, and then insist on testing for results. The search for magic teaching bullets is delusional. It includes class size, one of the latest. Research clearly shows smaller classes produce better results. Except I'd rather have Mr. Eckler teach a class of 40 than someone else with 20. Four hundred years ago, a teaching authority, Comenius, said the ideal student-teacher ratio was 300-1. He probably had research to prove it. There is no ideal ratio. In general, smaller may be better, but don't get dogmatic, trust the teacher. What works, works.

What's striking about most current educational reforms is how they try to interfere with what teachers do when the door closes. The advocates don't often say they're interfering, they say they want to help teachers and add, "There is no one best way." Then they list dozens, or more, of specifics for teachers to do. In the U.S., there are commercially purchased scripts that aim to have all teachers in a district on the same page at the same time. There's a 357-page tome unofficially known as Lemov's Taxonomy (by educator Doug Lemov) loaded with specifics like, "Stand still when you're giving directions." It had "hundreds of underground fans," according to The New York Times, even before it was published last spring. The effect of standardized tests like those known as EQAO (since they're administered by the Education Quality and Accountability Office of the Ontario Ministry of Education) is, says U.S. author Richard Rothstein, "to invade the classroom" and force teachers to "teach to the test," while cutting down on everything else.

I have some sympathy for the impulse to interfere. Leaving teachers on their own with your kids and their futures can be scary. It's like the trust you hand over to surgeons when they put you under. But teachers are professionals too, aren't they? That's the alternative attitude. You see it in Finland. Since the Organization for Economic Cooperation and Development (OECD) began ranking countries in 2000 for student achievement on Program for International Student Assessment (PISA) tests, it's been the star performer. It always scores at or near the top in all categories.

My biggest surprise there was the staffrooms. They took me in for coffee, a national passion. But in just about each one, there was a group of teachers, often with a principal, discussing an educational issue. At my first school, in Helsinki, it was about Facebook. Teachers send daily emails to parents about material covered in class. But some kids got their parents' passwords and copied the emails to Facebook, with wicked comments. A day later, up north in Kokkala, it was about cattiness among ten-year-old girls. Next day, elsewhere, it was teasing. There's a national policy on teasing and they were debating how to apply it.

I started wondering if these discussions were staged to impress visitors. I've seen Canadian staffrooms but don't recall such meetings, seemingly cheerful and voluntary. I think of Canadian teachers using staffrooms to chill out. Anyone who raises a classroom issue might get the evil eye. Discussions happen but elsewhere, in the hall or over in the corner. Back home, I checked with people who confirmed it. Every teacher and principal I described it to, did some kind of jaw-drop. I mentioned it to Toronto District School Board director Chris Spence, a pretty on-message guy not given to outbursts. "Unsolicited??!!" he blurted, as if he couldn't believe those discussions were voluntary.

How do they "incentivize" this teacher engagement in Finland? They don't. Teaching is the incentive. It is high prestige, higher than doctors, lawyers and architects. Last year there were ten applicants for every university position in teaching programs, which get to "cherry pick" from the top 20 percent of high school grads. There are entrance exams and interviews, plus a "teaching-like" activity in which they're observed to see if they have the right stuff. The training averages from five to seven and a half years – and is comparable to other professional degrees. All teachers must have a Master's degree and do a thesis. There are no separate teachers' colleges or certification programs. The university degree is the license to teach. With this training, teachers can readily transfer into jobs at private firms like Nokia. When asked what might make them want to leave, teachers don't say loss of pay; their pay is pretty much the national average and similar to other countries. But a loss of autonomy would make them consider getting out. What matters is their sense of professional control and responsibility.

What caused this commitment to teacher autonomy? Peter Johnson, Kokkola's education director, says it's bred into the national character. Finns fought for "autonomy" within the Russian empire, fought a civil war, fought for independence, resisted the Soviet invasion and fought to get the Germans out of Lapland. Autonomy is the national cry of honour, and it seeps into fields like teaching. "How else can you account for this element in our school system?" says Johnson, as if he's a lifelong learner himself, who loves searching for "causes." A sense of autonomy pervades the whole system. High school isn't compulsory, but Finland has a grad rate of 93 percent compared to 76 percent in Canada and 77 percent in the U.S. Membership in the teachers' union is voluntary but 96-97 percent join and pay dues directly; there's no "check-off," or automatic deduction, as there is here. It would be surprising if this air of autonomy and self-government didn't extend to classrooms and students.

And in fact Finnish teachers spend fewer hours in class than other teachers: the equivalent of four 45-minute classes daily in the middle grades – about half as much as U.S. teachers, and well under the average in comparable (OECD) countries. Classes tend to be small – from 15 to 30 in the lower grades – but there are no minimum or maximum sizes. Teachers get roughly equal time to do other things, like lesson prep, helping design curriculum or school renovations, and for those staffroom dialogues. They're trusted to use the time well because they're dedicated professionals in a "learning community."

Students too have a lighter load. They don't start school till age seven. Their class time and homework are among the lowest in the OECD countries. It's another of those counter-intuitives, but nations whose students spend fewer hours in class, like Finland, Korea or Japan, do better according to the PISA international test scores than those with far higher levels, like Italy, Portugal and Greece. By age 14, for instance, Finnish kids will have fewer than 6,000 hours in school versus Italian kids at over 8,000. This also goes for homework. Those high-achieving Finnish 15-year-olds spend less time on it than their peers elsewhere.

Social prestige and self-respect are of course hard things to nail down objectively. I recall, from my own years in school, a feeling that some of our teachers bore a hidden wound, as if they knew the deference they got from us would dissipate when we became adults ourselves. When I clumsily asked some Finnish teachers if they felt highly respected, they laughed and said "No." But an hour later, at lunch, when I asked what they do in the case of a bad teacher, the answer was: "We have very good teachers." It sounded almost cocky, given the modest, reticent Finnish manner. I don't think you'd hear that in Canada.

At the Toronto conference I mentioned, Annie Kidder, of the grassroots group People for Education, asked Finnish educator and author Pasi Sahlberg about "the parent piece" in Finland. He said, more or less, that it doesn't exist, and parents like him don't worry about it because they trust teachers and the system. It felt shocking, even irresponsible, in our context. But context is crucial. In the Finnish context, there's good reason to trust one's fellow citizens, based on experiences like relative economic equality and a generous safety net. Elsewhere it might be harder, like the U.S., where the attitude to teachers, said one educator, is "Bring it!" – meaning high test scores. In U.S. society, there's so little general trust and so much pervasive fear, it's hard to picture anything remotely Finnish. Canada, as usual, falls somewhere in between.

But public school classrooms are also places where those attitudes get formed. Donald Eckler says:

> Parents forget what school was like. They think it's about learning things. But it's far more a community. I can't really define what I'm doing, but I want it to be an environment that's comfortable and respectful. What it feels like to me is a family. People get hurt, others open up space for them. Kids are so kind to the kid who has Asperger's. All that is far more important than curriculum. What they're really learning is how to co-exist in that environment and what learning means.

Think again about learning to read. Teachers say when kids who've been doing something together are asked to open a book and read, they vanish into their own private worlds. Then they pull out of it again. That's the essence of being human: you're both social and individual. Fine teachers sense that this in itself is a lesson – or the lesson.

It seems to me you can basically choose to give teachers the autonomy to make such moments frequent, or you can try to intervene in their classrooms (while denying it) in the hope that you can drive up test scores, or whatever obsesses you. I don't think the Finnish model is foolproof, but it seems, at the least, like a more interesting and adult way to go.

Two afterthoughts:

• My most memorable teacher was Nehama Labovitz. She taught me Bible when I was a student in Israel. She looked like Old Dutch from Old Dutch cleanser and taught everyone from refugees in camps to grad students. As with most superb teachers, her method didn't fit a formula and is hard to describe. It often involved citing a cryptic, one- or two-word Hebrew phrase from a medieval Bible commentator and asking: "What was bothering him?" Then drawing help from anywhere she could get it. She's the first person I ever heard mention the great Canadian critic Northrop Frye. "He's wrong," she said, "but you must read him." She sometimes took me home to feed me since she knew I spent most of what I had buying those multi-volume commentaries she got me hooked on. She flew under the radar of rabbinic authorities for years, though they eventually tried to shut her down. She said a traditional Jewish saying claimed teachers went straight to heaven since they'd experienced a lot of hell on earth. But she disagreed; as a teacher, she'd already had more than her fair share of heaven.

• Bob Bevan is principal of Tommy Douglas High School in Saskatoon. He says he once placed headshots of all the students in his school along a hallway. Then he had each teacher put a red dot on the photos of kids they had a substantial personal relationship with. He says there were kids who had 40 or 50 dots. But there were hundreds with no dots. The main way to improve achievement in the school was clear: Connect with those kids.

II. Against Choice

It isn't easy arguing against school choice. Let me try to make the case, using Toronto as an example that has provided a wide and impressive variety within the public system.

There wasn't always much choice in the Toronto system. You went to your local school, right through high school. You might take an extra language or music course. And there was the vocational "stream." End of choices. Now you can be in French immersion from senior kindergarten. Or in a gifted program or in alternative schools. You could choose an arts high school, among several. There are schools for cyberarts, entrepreneurialism, integrated technology and the international baccalaureate. There's an Africentric school and there may soon be "academies" for boys, girls, choirs and jocks. Some are stand-alone, some are independent but in existing schools, some are part of regular schools. Even in early years, you can apply for a school outside your local area. Admission procedures vary almost case by case; some are competitive, some by lottery. My question is: do we lose as well as gain with this much choice?

Let me do a quick cut-to-the-chase by way of charter schools in the U.S. They aren't the same but they're the ultimate version of school choice there, which is how they're sold. (They're the schools hailed in the highly promoted documentary film "Waiting for Superman.") They're paid for by public funds but run privately. They amount to privatizing the public system on the public dime, topped up by foundation and corporate money. Statistically, they do no better and often worse than the public schools they badmouth. In math, in 2009, 17 percent of charters posted scores better than comparable public schools, while 37 percent were "significantly below." They're at best a quick fix for the few. But they can and do drain the life out of the public system there and leave it even more of a demoralized shell than it is now. That's the risk in going hell-bent for choice: you undermine the only real choice for most families: public schools.

Michael Barber was a key player in education "reform" in the U.K. during the Blair years. He now acts as an international consultant; among those he advises is Ontario Premier Dalton McGuinty. He says we need to "bind" the rich to the public schools via reforms like Choice or they'll desert it for private schools, and "full-scale privatization" could follow. Toronto District School Board director Chris Spence echoes this when he says we need to establish separate "academies" to offer "what have traditionally been private school opportunities within the public system." Yet those choices, if they happen, will peel off some of the best principals and teachers, along with vocal parents who'd otherwise exert pressure for system-wide improvement. Spence says it's "about retaining and attracting students," but at what cost? At the cost of cannibalizing and undermining the mainstream schools?

These are the real dangers in these special schools and programs:

• They break down cohesion in local communities and neighbourhoods by sending kids scuttling all over the city. Toronto's strength lies in its neighbourhoods, and schools are a big part of that.

• They deprive kids of the stimulation of different types of minds, experiences and skills, in the same classrooms.

- They take pressure off the system to improve for all kids by giving certain insistent groups what they demand.

- They take the wrong direction: fragmentation rather than integration.

Oh and by the way, if you "control" for things like income, private schools do no better than public ones. The same kids get the same marks in either. Let me take a quick tour of some of these "choice" or specialty schools along with their actual and potential downsides.

French Immersion

It's the exemplary special program. Kids in French immersion learn French, but all others, despite taking French daily starting in Grade 4, often learn practically no French. If there were no French immersion, parents whose kids now take it would be screaming for better results. Learning another language is a kind of breakthrough skill, fruitful in many ways; Ontario has effectively abandoned it except for immersion. In New Brunswick, where bilingualism is like a civic creed, they've cancelled French immersion because, according to then education minister Kelly Lamrock, it created a two-tier segregated system and helped drag down the overall scores (not just in French) of the vast majority of kids in public schools.

"Alternative" schools

Many of these began in response to middle-class parents who wanted individualized treatment for their kids in smaller settings. They often have a precious, elite quality. You feel it at their open houses: an implication that if you stick with the main system, you'll be warehoused with the masses. "This reverses the traditional dynamic of public schools," said one teacher, "which immigrant and working class families saw as a road to integration and advancement."

"Gifted" programs

These involve separate classes for "brighter" kids, based on tests for verbal and spatial skills. Middle-class parents often push for their kids to take these tests; as a result, those kids may be over-represented. It's an unfortunate term since all kids are gifted. (That isn't rhetoric; I'd call it a fact.) Some of these kids also fit the learning disabilities (LD) category. Whenever possible, LD (and developmentally disabled) kids are integrated in regular classrooms, and it works well. It may not help kids who are both "gifted" and LD to mark them off doubly. Besides, there are many forms of intelligence. They can complement each other. I don't see the value of isolating some modes from others. It's possible to accommodate different approaches for different kids in the same class, where they can learn from each other. In classrooms with skilful (or gifted) teachers, you often can't tell if you're in one or the other.

Arts schools

Personally, I dislike the cult of the artist, and art, because it separates art from everyday life and "ordinary" people. Of the four arts high schools in Toronto – there are also five elementary arts schools and several "programs" – the one with the least artsy quality is Rosedale Heights.

It doesn't audition; anyone can go; you get no advantage because your folks could afford lessons. Barrie Sketchley, its veteran principal, didn't start with an arts agenda. When he went there, it had been a vocational school. The NDP government of the time wanted to try bringing together kids who'd been "streamed" in separate academic or vocational directions. But, Sketchley says, you needed some cachet to attract kids. They settled on arts. He'd always loved the arts but his real drive was to "create a place for vulnerable kids with an air of acceptance." He says the level of achievement may not be as high as at "audition" schools, though many kids are talented and the place buzzes with theatre, dance, etc. In a sense he's created a separate arts school without much sense of separation. In a system with a deep-rooted feel for culture, the arts would be equally available to all kids in all schools, but this is a start.

Africentric

For decades, African-Canadian parents demanded help for underachieving kids and got nowhere. Almost any effort would be justified as a remedy, and this school has already produced decent results on provincial tests: its 16 Grade 3 students outscored both Toronto and Ontario averages. But Toronto teacher Lisa Guthro, who just moved from a poor to a middle-class school, says, "Ask my new students about Africa and they say: Who lives there? They need courses on Africa as much as those kids do." I know my own kid would love it. He's fascinated by tales of slavery and freedom. Wouldn't it be good for African-Canadian kids to see his admiration for their past? Besides, special schools will never serve to raise the level of all the kids in need; and the Africentric school may have removed some of the strongest parental pressure for action. You can make a better case for this alternative school than the others, but the "logic of choice" works to undercut the wider system here too.

Boys' academies

This means setting up separate schools for boys only. Toronto School Board director Chris Spence is their main promoter; they haven't been implemented yet. He's written a book recommending them, in which he bases a large part of his claim that boys and girls learn differently on observations of his own kids and their friends ("Little girls… flirt, they pout, they manipulate."). Much of his reasoning ("Boys are sensitive to teacher disapproval") would apply to both genders. He cites an experiment when he headed the Hamilton board but it was only with two classes for one year; the evaluation was limited to a grad student's interviews with eight kids and a follow-up survey of 62 kids. He acknowledges that "overall, students did not rate the single-gender experience favourably," but he still maintains, "the idea of all male classes and schools make sense." He's relied on a U.S. author, Leonard Sax, a psychologist and family physician, whose views have been disputed by other experts there, largely on whether Sax makes too much of small differences in learning between boys and girls. The critics say the differences among boys are larger than those between boys and girls. Spence himself concedes, "the debate … goes on, and there is evidence to support both arguments." Yet he wants to push ahead strongly on this front, not just with boys' academies but other types. It seems likely his real motive is to do something for ill-served, mostly black "inner city kids," for whom "radical measures are in order." He'd have done better to just say that. Instead it's as if he chose to bolster his case with arguments about gender and choice, then to sweeten it with other academies – 16 in all, for girls, choirs, athletes etc. That could open the way to even more "choices" that might ultimately include, say, religious schools or charter-like private schools paid for with public funds. That would drain further funds and talented personnel away from the mainstream schools where most kids, inevitably, will be found.

The alternative that never was

In the 1990s, surveys showed that kids of Portuguese, working-class background in Toronto weren't achieving at the levels of other groups. Some principals, trustees etc., thought it might help if some of them attended alternative schools for Grades 7-8. But when they spoke to the parents, "their eyes glazed over." The idea of travelling across the city to attend open houses and shop for schools was foreign to them. If they did make the trek, they saw no one who looked like them. The emphasis shifted to creating an alternative school for them in their own neighbourhood, at Grace Street Public School, which had declining enrolment and space on its third floor. But that faltered for similar reasons. Like the fact that alternative schools depend on an active parent base to fundraise and assist in classes – a "skill set" which working- class immigrants largely lacked, along with the time to do it, given their work hours. Eventually the alternative got going, at another school in another area. It's now called City View and continues to thrive, but mostly with a population drawn from a better off, more vocal demographic it wasn't originally aimed at. As for Grace Street, it closed, and turned into Pierre Elliott Trudeau Elementary French School. So the chattering classes wound up with not one but two more special schools, after a noble, unsuccessful effort.

Many teachers and principals seem pragmatic about most of these programs. They've seen flavours of the month come and go in education. If it helps some kids with particular needs or interests – why not?

But could you respond to those needs and talents without fragmenting and undermining the larger system? Yes, you could: by sending the programs into each school, instead of scattering the kids to centralized programs. A model for that in the Toronto system is Special Ed.

For kids with especially serious disabilities, there are separate, wonderfully humane places like the Beverley School. But whenever possible, these kids go into mainstream schools, either in separate classes or in "normal" classrooms. Either way, they're part of a larger school community. It benefits all kids, not just Special Ed kids, and is one of the glories of the system. You could say it anticipates other forms of inclusiveness not yet achieved.

This goes for kids with behavioural and discipline problems too. I once saw a kid kill a butterfly in a schoolyard after school. It had been bred in his class. Parents looking on were furious and said so. But his classmates were less judgmental; they knew his home situation and his constant need for attention (unlike the attention the butterfly received, though they didn't put it that way). Making an issue of his act, they said, would only aggravate things. It's that kind of empathetic insight into your society that an inclusive school can deliver.

In Finland, which has an extraordinarily successful public system, Special Ed kids go into mainstream schools very early; the Finns say this builds social cohesion and raises achievement levels. Saskatchewan has a category called "community schools." It aims to meld the two terms. Rather than sending kids elsewhere to meet special needs concerning, say, alcohol or violence, they put the social service workers right in local schools, where they work with teachers and go into classrooms. The problems get normalized and discussed there by everyone rather than stigmatized and ostracized. I think the same could hold for kids with special talents: mix them in, rather than separating them out.

John Dewey wrote, in "Democracy and Education," that private schools may have a social spirit, but it's no more like the real world beyond school walls than is the social spirit in a monastery. We risk that kind of narrowness by cloistering kids in special programs and schools.

Let me try to make the point by way of the definitive separate program in Canadian public education: publicly funded Catholic schools. They're so separate they are their own system. That has to do with the roots of Canadian history and the deal made between French and English populations to create Canada, not with recent ideas about school choice. But there are elements in the Catholic tradition that would be useful in any school, religious or not. I heard an Ottawa Catholic school official tell a meeting that, when it comes to hiring principals, "Everyone wants Jesus Christ with computer skills." The whole room perked up. He had access to a set of images that non-religious people don't; it helped put things in perspective.

I met a principal at a Regina Catholic school who said every night she asks herself if she treated each student as a Christ child that day. At another, a principal said when he deals with fighting, he might ask kids if they feel this is a Christian way to act. The morning Bible lesson (over the PA) at a Regina inner-city Catholic school, was about the love that surrounds us even when we're unaware of it. In the broad, open way it was phrased, it would have made as much sense to the non-Catholic kids there as to the Catholic majority. You don't need to be Catholic, or even religious, to get the point of these images.

I don't see why you couldn't, over time, integrate Catholic and other spiritual sensibilities into the public system, in an open-minded, tolerant way. We need all the resources we can get, and so do our kids. Someone I know says her daughter saw a Bible and asked, "What's a 'bibble?'" It enriches kids to know about "bibbles" of various religions and worldviews. It may just be fantasy at this point, but I can imagine reintegrating "separate" schools into the public system without totally defrocking them, to everyone's benefit. Maybe the dogma parts could be kept aside for Sunday school or – well, I haven't worked it all out yet.

People sometimes sound guilty or apologetic about sending kids to private schools. I think that's a non-issue. As a parent, you do what seems best for your kids. But as a citizen, you should support the public system and help strengthen it where it's weak. The question is: How do you do that? Is it by cutting it up into bite-size pieces and trying to accommodate every taste separately? Or is it by emphasizing the unique strength of the public system: its inclusiveness – the stimulating variety it provides to all kids when they meet and get to know each other?

Trying to save public schools by chopping them to bits and "privatizing from within" is like destroying the village in order to save it. Maybe there should be a Hippocratic oath for educators, like the one for doctors: First, do no harm.

III. Testing, testing ... You're fired!

If your kid recently soldiered through any of the proliferating number of standardized tests, like Ontario's EQAO tests in reading, math and science, for Grades 3, 6 and 9, then you've been part of a worldwide "homogenization" of education techniques. This kind of testing is meant less to measure how kids are doing, than how their teachers and schools are doing, so that they can be held "accountable." Now there's nothing wrong with accountability. And testing is a necessary teaching tool. The problem is accountability based on high-stakes, standardized tests.

Standardized means the same for everybody, set by a central authority — a government department or private company. But kids aren't the same. A test can tell you what a kid scores, not what the score means for the kid. That depends on where she started from, what his abilities are and what's important for her to know. A low mark for one kid might be a better sign than a high mark for another of the same age. Teachers know these things and can adjust the lesson (and the mark's meaning) to the learner. But anonymous test scorers being paid per exam marked, can't. So standardized tests are poor indicators of how kids and teachers are doing.

It gets worse when you tack the accountability piece onto standardized testing, as they've done all over the U.S. It may seem plausible and clear-cut. But when test scores become the basis for rewards and punishments like hiring, firing, teacher pay, and school funding or closing, the tests grow vulnerable to (and even "create an incentive for") cheating: by getting tests in advance and giving them to kids, gaming the system in ways like shifting pass/fail levels, faking results, or "counselling out" weaker students so the school or class average rises.

All this is documented in U.S. education historian Diane Ravitch's book, The Death and Life of the Great American School System. She gets credibility because she served as a high official under George W. Bush, bringing in and arguing for the approach. She now says "we were wrong ... testing actually makes the schools worse." Any learning gains made are shaky and can "evaporate" quickly once the testing pressure is off. Learning in a school can even decline because of testing. There's a technical term for it: Campbell's Law, proclaimed by U.S. expert in methodology David Campbell. It says if you base accountability on measurements, what you're measuring may get worse instead of better. It sounds weird but it happens, for instance, if ERs are rated by number of patients treated quickly: they might rush people through rather than provide good care, in order to raise their score. So you're better off not going there despite its high rank.

The list of objections is almost endless. The saddest come from teachers; many are cited by former New York Times education columnist Richard Rothstein in his book on accountability. They're painful to read, the way TV crime dramas about child abuse can be painful to watch. Teachers say they now lack time to do things they loved, like taking kids on trips, or teaching trigonometry by going outside and measuring shadows in the sun. It all loses out to prepping for tests.

Besides, as John Dewey said, nothing kills the joy of learning like failing to have a real-life reason for the lesson. If you're told you need it for a test, or as training for something later in life, it drains the life and joy from the present, and kids specialize in the present. If you're not having fun, it's really hard to learn, says a kid I know. That probably goes for teachers too.

Are there other ways to assess teachers and schools than numerical test scores? Yes, there have been many; they just aren't as easy to measure. The U.K. began obsessively quantifying during the Thatcher years, but it still sent teams into schools to evaluate various items beyond test scores until the 1990s. In its early years, the U.S. National Assessment of Educational Progress, NAEP, used a wide range of methodologies to judge success. If you take the trouble, you can assess outcomes in areas like personal growth, civics, health, or art. You can judge by essays, artwork, physical challenges or public service. An Australian evaluation asked kids: Are there political causes worth fighting for? What a great question to judge whether a school successfully "taught" a sense of civic responsibility. In fact, current fixations on "measurables" to the exclusion of everything else start to look like aberrations from the long-term trend.

I know that testing for reading, writing and math sounds like the three Rs – the basics – from the good old days of public education. But Egerton Ryerson, Canada's great advocate of public schools in the 19th century, had a larger role in mind for the system he largely created in Ontario. He wanted schools to counter the anti-monarchy and republican influences that came with heavy immigration from the U.S. and that led to the rebellion of 1837; plus, to construct an Anglo balance to the French fact in Quebec. This amounted to a "citizenship" agenda that inculcated moral values, alongside the training he wanted to provide for every child.

In the U.S., founding fathers like Franklin and Jefferson also supported public education for moral and civic ends, not just or even mainly for academic skills that would be useful in the work force. In 1830 a Pennsylvania committee warned that poor and working children should get more than "a simple acquaintance with words and ciphers."

They should also acquire "a just disposition, virtuous habits and a rational, self-governing character." All this is what we now think of as character education or a citizenship agenda. In the 1930s, John Dewey said it was important not just to know how to read, but to know how to distinguish between the "demagogue and the statesman." In fact, in the old days, all in all, there was probably less emphasis on "the basics" than there is now. The basics didn't used to be so basic.

Then how did the notion of accountability grow so narrow that it is increasingly correlated with scores on tests? Partly, it suited the business culture of our era, which prefers anything that can be quantified down to a fine powder. Bill Gates, in his new incarnation as education expert, says any teaching that you can't measure is useless. (I wonder how you'd measure that claim.) The testing at certain points becomes manic. The U.K. under Thatcher reported on about 1,000 skills per kid, leading eventually to a huge revolt by teachers and headmasters. The U.S. version was George Bush's No Child Left Behind, followed by Barack Obama's Race to the Top. The latter program sent millions in extra funding to Washington, D.C. schools, partly because of their high test scores. Teachers and principals also received individual bonuses. But those scores are now under investigation because of abnormally high rates of "erasures" — wrong answers being rubbed out and replaced with correct answers on computerized tests. And in Atlanta, a huge scandal involving teachers and principals who "cheated on standardized tests to inflate student scores" was revealed. The system's boss, who was named National Superintendent of the Year in 2009, covered up and punished whistleblowers, going back to 2001 – all apparently due to "pressure to meet score targets."

In Canada, the obsessiveness hasn't gone as far. But we're partway down that road. A small but apparently potent unit in Ontario called the Literacy and Numeracy Secretariat has been set up in the education ministry. Its mandate is to improve teaching generally, but people in the field say it's pretty relentlessly focused on boosting those EQAO scores. In a way, once the tests exist, it's hard not to fix on them. They're so concrete; they tend to take over from other forms of assessment. Education officials are very good at verbalizing lofty "show goals" like teaching civics or creativity; it helps give all the testing a more human face. But they tend to put their fervour into hailing the latest scores.

It hasn't reached the point, as in the U.S. that they're the basis for hiring, firing or funding. But they do serve to guide parents in choosing (and rejecting) schools. Ontario has a "School Information Finder" that gives EQAO results and socio-economic strata data for parents to check. Premier Dalton McGuinty came under pressure to dismantle it but refused. He wouldn't want to look soft on "basics" like tough testing, which polling shows support for, in a right-leaning era. So politically, he treads carefully.

There is some recent resistance to the testing-accountability recipe. In the U.K., the "Celtic fringe" – Scotland, Wales and Northern Ireland – are dropping or limiting standardized tests. Even England has canned them for the early grades, after a revolt including strike threats by headmasters in 2009. As for us, B.C. was big on the tests but has recently wobbled about whether they'll be imposed, in response to objections from parents, teachers and principals.

The most intriguing counter-case is Finland. Since the Organization for Economic Cooperation and Development began ranking countries in 2000 by their scores on the international PISA tests, it's been the star performer. PISA is the Programme for International Student Assessment. It measures educational achievement in the 30 or so OECD members, though it also surveys other countries and some cities. Every three years it tests five thousand 15-year-old students per country, in Reading, Mathematics and Science, with special emphasis on one of those for each round. The tests are handwritten; partly multiple-choice and partly short essays. There is also a questionnaire on background, study habits etc. Then it sifts and compares results. Its methods are highly regarded. The first three test years (2000, 2003, 2006) showed Finland at the top in that year's main category. Canada did well, placing second twice and fifth once. In 2009, Finland scored first or second in all categories among OECD members. Canada was fifth, fifth and third. Some countries have done surprisingly poorly; the U.S. and Germany were generally in the middle or at the back of the pack.

Yet Finland, which always scores at or near the top in all categories, does no standardized testing till the very end of high school ("the first and last national test," says a teacher in Helsinki). So the results have shocked everyone, starting with the Finns. Their country shot onto everyone's list of most successful countries, especially since it also leads in prosperity (according to the British think tank, Legatum, 2009); competitiveness (World Economic Forum, 2003-5); and perceived lack of corruption (Transparency International, 2010). Delegations of educators and journalists began arriving in the tens of thousands. Literally. When I entered staffrooms there, teachers kind of rolled their eyes, then got helpful. It especially miffed them since they don't value being number one on tests and didn't aim for it. "We hate those results," says Pasi Sahlberg, the prominent author/educator who has represented Finland at the World Bank, the OECD, the E.U. and elsewhere. "It's not a competition, it's about building community," he says. They do enjoy beating out Sweden, which ruled them for centuries. But that's it.

Their big school reform began 40 years ago and wasn't about scores; it was about creating a single school model for all students up to high school. Till then, students had been "streamed" in academic or vocational directions. In other words the reform was about diminishing school "choice" for the sake of greater equality and social unity. There was a long, raucous debate. Many people, including teachers, argued against the reform, saying it would lower standards. The 2000 PISA results finally ended that debate. Everyone could see the reforms weren't only socially just; they were academically brilliant.

There's no obvious reason why Finland's approach yields such great scores. I sat with a university researcher in the small city of Kokkala, 200 km south of the Arctic Circle, as she explained her theory about why Finland's approach yields such great scores. But all she really did was restate the elements of the Finnish approach, like teacher autonomy and an emphasis on social equality, without explaining why they produced those results. Her assumption was: Our system must be the cause of those effects.

So here's my theory: Everyone knows that what tests really test is how good you are at taking tests. The tenser you are, the lower you're likely to score. Since Finns don't worry about tests, they're loose going in, and score well. This jibes with a report that found only 7 percent of Finnish students feel anxiety doing Math homework versus 52 percent and 53 percent for French and Japanese kids.

It's not that Finns don't test. They just don't do standardized, "high-stakes" tests. There were lots of tests in classrooms I visited, and in the halls, where individual kids or small groups might be taking tests with the aid of a teacher or assistant. But teachers set the tests themselves. They do it, one told her students, "because I want to know how you've learned and I want to know how I've taught." Most good teachers I know feel this way: they value tests, as long as they exist to serve the learning process, and not vice versa.

As for accountability, the Finns also reject rewards and punishment based on externally set performance targets. Peter Johnson, director of education for Kokkala, (whose job includes museums, libraries, youth sports, and filling in for the mayor when he's away) says with quiet pride, "Finland saw its last inspector in 1985." We were having dinner in late November. It was dark and cold outside. The sun rose about 10:30 a.m. and set four hours later. "We believe in self-evaluation," he went on. He called it inside-out or self-service accountability. Others call it smart accountability. They agree with assessing success based on results. They just don't think test scores should be the results used. They also think self-assessment is faster and more efficient. If you find a problem, you fix it. You don't have to wait for inspection reports. Peter Johnson said he once told this to a group of 30 visiting Europeans. "They were so silent." Then one asked if it were true Finland has no inspectors. It suddenly occurred to Johnson to ask if any of them were inspectors, and "half raised their hands."

This may sound odd to Canadians. Why should anyone trust teachers with self-accountability? When Ontario teachers criticized the EQAO tests, a Globe and Mail editorial said, "They don't wish to be held accountable." That's the common, U.S.-style response: attack teachers. Finland shows there are other kinds of accountability. Their version relies on the rest of society trusting educators. But how do you get to that level of trust? I'll return to this question later.

When I mention Finland to educators here or in the U.S., they're often dismissive. They say it's not comparable: It's too small (5.3 million), white, homogeneous and middle class. But it does far better than comparable Scandinavian nations like Norway and Denmark, so something more is going on than size and uniformity. Its diversity is also increasing due to E.U. membership; its foreign-born citizens have doubled in the last decade. There are schools with more than 40 percent immigrant students; in Helsinki (pop. 580,000) schools have 40 percent immigrant kids and over 40 languages spoken. Based on PISA data, those kids perform better than immigrant kids in similar places, so again, Finland is doing something right.

As for size, education is controlled by Canadian provinces and U.S. states so it's fair to compare to them rather than the whole country: Finland is smaller than Ontario and Quebec but bigger than the other provinces, many of which are pretty homogeneous. Finland is also a northern land that was historically dominated by larger powers, like us. Its obsession, like ours, was Survival. It makes as much – no, greater – sense to compare ourselves to them, rather than to imperial behemoths like the U.S. and the U.K., which are massively dissimilar. Besides, to get to Finland from Canada, you fly for endless hours, and when you arrive, it feels as though you never left here.

There are differences, of course. Finland has few resources aside from fresh water and trees. From this they concluded they have to be smart and well-educated to succeed economically, which they've done. Even from this difference, I'd say we can learn something: that being resource-rich, like us, can make you stupid and slow off the mark, just as tests can dull young minds.

Nor are the people I met there complacent. "I fear this will all end badly," says Pasi Sahlberg, meaning the hoo-ha about Finnish test scores. He thinks the E.U. will use Finland's educational success as a reason to REDUCE some economic benefits it now receives. He also has darker fears: that the passion for justice and independence that motivated the reforms will wane, its place inadequately filled by some fickle international acclaim and admiring foreign delegations. Finland is currently sending consultants and teachers to help in Abu Dhabi. Peter Johnson says, "We had inequality and built our system on overcoming it; why should we help rich countries instead of those in real need?" What will inspire future generations of Finnish educators? Sahlberg and Johnson both wonder.

The point was never to score high on international tests; the point was fairness and equity. Yet their test scores zoomed up anyway. It's as if the best way to improve your marks is to forget about them and focus on doing the right thing. It's like happiness; you don't get it by aiming for it, but it sometimes happens on the way to somewhere else.

Meanwhile Canada's provinces continue along the course of standardized testing, little concerned, it appears, about the perils and precedents. We could use a little of that Finnish malaise over the value of testing, along with their absence of complacency about the future.

IV. Equity: Who Are "We" Now?

From its 19th century beginnings in Ontario, universal Canadian public education was a venture in equity, which is another way to say fairness. The "public" then was mostly white and Protestant, with British or American roots. But the rich among them had their own private schools. Public schools arose to equalize access to schooling.

The public grew more complex through immigrant waves: German, Jewish, Italian, etc. They often arrived poor, spoke other languages and didn't know "our" public values. The schools taught their kids those values along with the skills to raise themselves economically. As prosperity came, the values tended to follow. So public education was an exercise in assimilation, and it generally worked. Public schools created public citizens.

More recent immigrants pose additional challenges. Most aren't white and many aren't Christian (or Judaeo-Christian). Some arrive wealthy but lots don't. The traditional route to integration and Canadianization has been through the public schools. But not all kids thrive there; African-Canadian boys are a striking example, particularly in Toronto, but kids from other backgrounds – Latin American, Portuguese, Vietnamese, for example – are also struggling. The schools haven't been doing their traditional job for these groups.

There is also the festering case of aboriginal peoples, which raises this issue across the country. In the more or less distant past, they were expected to assimilate through the school system, because their own communities were considered primitive and backward. That simply isn't on now.

The question is: What happens when the "public" in public education changes? It now includes these new "racialized" groups, and it includes Canada's first inhabitants. You can't eliminate either from your definition of public, the way you once could – but some of them are being ill-served in the public schools. It doesn't mean the whole system is failing but it does mean it isn't truly public. If we think that matters, what can be done? Let me consider two examples, one from each of these constituencies.

Pathways to Education is a shockingly effective program for high school kids that began in Regent Park, a low-income, public housing area in Toronto. It's 80 percent non-white with English as a second language, and known for gangs and violence. Pathways was started in 2001 by Carolyn Acker, who had been a community health nurse there. She says she used to go home at night feeling, "All I am is a band-aid." She and others decided to "break the cycle of poverty" by lowering the high-school dropout rate. They did this by basically ignoring the schools, or accepting them as they are, and focusing maniacally on the kids.

They began by giving out bus fare to get to school. It had been cut under the government of Mike Harris in Ontario during the 1990s. If kids don't show at school, they don't get the fare. Many kids figured out you could keep the money if you left early and walked, which they proceeded to do. Pathways put $1,000 a year per kid into an account for post-secondary studies each year that the kids remain in school. The kids are assigned workers who keep tabs on them. They get regular tutoring. Attendance is mandatory. They sign contracts each year to uphold their end. The annual budget for the Regent Park program is about $4.5 million; all of it has to be raised, some from government agencies but a lot from other sources, including fundraising, much of it from big financial firms on Bay Street, which love the program. They don't just give money, they provide mentors and jobs.

In the first five years the dropout rate in Regent Park dived from 56 percent to 10 percent. Post-secondary attendance rose from 21 percent to 80 percent. Out of more than 1,000 kids from Regent Park who attend various Toronto high schools, 93 percent now graduate. The program has now expanded to 11 communities from Halifax to Winnipeg. It involves 3,400 students and costs $4,800 per year per student. About 60-70 percent of its costs are funded by provincial and federal governments, the rest comes from private and non-government sources. The separate programs are independently run but overseen by a national body.

Ghissan (not his real name; he doesn't want his parents to know what he was once into) had been in a Regent Park gang. "You beat up guys, you get beat up, you make good money delivering drugs for dealers but you can get put away for ten years." He heard about Pathways and got involved. He left the gang, gradually, so as not to upset his pals. Now he's doing an MA in social work. He switched over from a marketing program; he says you make more money that way but he hated being stuck in a cubicle. He wants to return to the area, work with kids and buy a house. He'd like to buy one for his parents too, in their South Asian homeland, because "they left everything for us." He says talk in Regent Park now isn't about gangs, it's where you'll do your MA. "If you only go to college, you get laughed at." The kids in university have started a Pathways alumni group. They donate to the program and figure that one day they'll "outnumber the kids in high school" so Pathways won't need to fundraise anymore. Talk about breaking the cycle.

This is opposite to the approach celebrated in the 2010 U.S. documentary, "Waiting for Superman," where broken public schools and bad teachers in them are seen as the problem — while the solution is private, publicly-funded "charter" schools. Those will never be a large-scale answer even if they work for a limited number. The typical counter-argument to "Waiting for Superman" and charter schools is that you can't help poor, underachieving kids unless you deal with the underlying causes of their poverty first. Pathways chooses neither of these routes. It doesn't try to transform the schools and it doesn't try to eliminate the poverty that damages the kids and their abilities. Instead it concentrates relentlessly on the kids at risk in high school and stays with them unshakably. What works is single-minded determination.

But Carolyn Acker says it wouldn't work for everyone. It's a "made-in-Canada solution," and not even for all of Canada. Pathways builds on the fact we have "a beautiful platform of social programs, we have outstanding elementary and high schools. You have that foundation and you use it." Toronto School Board director Chris Spence once asked, with undeniable moral passion, what we have to "celebrate" simply because "the kids who have always done well continue to do well." Pathways suggests an answer: Celebrate it, because you can build on it to make the needed repairs for those who are still struggling.

I went to Saskatchewan to see a different "equity" program that focuses on one ancient though diverse population: aboriginal peoples. It's like a reverse of Pathways: everything is drawn into the schools and all student needs are handled within them. It grew from the notion of "community schools," a fairly common educational term that usually denotes poor and "at-risk" populations. In Saskatchewan, the concept got updated more than ten years ago into something called SchoolPlus, which was unique because it meant to include not just schools with at-risk students but all the province's public schools, each in its own way according to its needs. The Brad Wall government that replaced the NDP in 2007 scrapped the name due to its association with the NDP but seems committed to the ideas behind it. The broadening to all schools hasn't happened, but about 100 of the 700 or so schools in the province are now designated "community," up from only 11 inner-city schools in 1999. They include high schools, rural and northern schools. Each gets about $140,000 in additional funds.

At venerable Nutana High in Saskatoon, with 60 percent aboriginal students, there's a huge range of services based right in the school. So kids don't face the stigma of being sent to see a social worker downtown "because you're screwed up." The service staff members work with classroom teachers and go into classes; issues like homelessness and alcoholism are handled right there. This "normalizes" them and makes them easier to discuss. There's a program for student-parents. I stupidly asked if that meant parents of students but it's for students who are parents. They bring their kids, including newborns, to school, visit between classes, learn to bond with them and get a credit in this (or in breastfeeding, or in fetal alcohol syndrome). One worker was a student here himself and at the time learned he was going to be a dad at the time. Now he runs the boys' mentorship group. A stay-in-school coordinator checks on kids who seem to have fallen off the face of the earth. They struggle to keep the kids "connected." Schools are supposed to cut students off at age 22 but Nutana accepts them till 28 or 29. They have Carolyn Acker's tenacity; it's the key ingredient.

At first it just looks like a grab bag of the usual services but assembled inside the schools. Then you realize it begins not with the services but with a community expressing what it needs, through some grassroots process. It might start with profiles written by the kids, which are then carefully analyzed. Or an entire school staff painstakingly figures out what's required in its community. Nothing is decreed from above and delivered from beyond. So the shape of each community school varies, depending on the needs of each community.

At Nutana it's mainly social services. At St. Mary's, also in Saskatoon, the stress is on health care because "the six blocks around here has the collective health profile of Uganda," says Gary Beaudin from the Catholic schools office, who works with the school. It's 100 years old, 90 percent aboriginal, and Catholic. They begin each week with a smudge – a native purification ritual – led by one of the two elders in residence. There's a pediatrician, a clinical psychologist, a dental hygienist, a kinesiology program and an optometrist they found who had "a social justice philosophy." Without that, say Beaudin and principal Tony Bairos, who went here himself as a kid, "it wouldn't work." They mean you need an extra level of commitment to work in this setting. Social justice philosophy isn't a category you run into a lot in Ontario, but in Saskatchewan it comes with the prairie socialism and co-op traditions. In Toronto, the equivalent might be the philanthropic mindset of Bay Street bankers who donate generously to Pathways.

Sacred Heart elementary in Regina, in what Maclean's called "the worst neighbourhood in Canada," focuses on safety and reading. December, when I visited, is rough. The kids see Christmas images that remind them of what they don't have; and there's often partying and drinking at home that they know can lead to violence. So they like to linger at school. But the place is also Reading Heaven. Kids read everywhere – in class, in the hallways – and they take computer tests to gain points for books they've read. There are family reading nights. Principal Starla Grebinski, who went here herself as a kid, competes with students in finishing books; often they're far ahead of her on points – "And sometimes they don't have heat or running water at home."

At Regina's Archbishop O'Neill High, they have "golden greeters" who come in every morning, seniors from the community who welcome the kids and create a mood that helps lower the incidence of hazing and conflict. They also teach cribbage, sewing, curling and power skating. The kids help clean up areas nearby. It builds an intergenerational community connection.

At Arcola Elementary in Regina, the main question asked by the staff was: "What will be good for our demographics?" Since they have the highest percentage of single families in Regina, they decided what they needed was, first, a sense of family and then, individualized instruction because the kids are at such different levels that one teacher per classroom isn't enough. So they concocted a program of team teaching, three or four teachers per expanded class. Some teachers resisted at first. Now you'd have to pry it out of their enthusiastic grip.

These schools have been "designated" community (formerly "SchoolPlus") schools, and with that comes the extra funding needed for what they do. But the community's own voice is at the centre. As a result you don't just end up giving the community what someone thinks it needs; you start changing the nature of the community and its schools.

This deeper level is explained by University of Regina education professor Michael Tymchak. He was the key figure behind the commission that made the proposals for change. He lays out a historical backdrop to the current situation. There was an original phase of fruitful contact out here between First Nations and arriving Europeans. Then came a long period when aboriginals "fell off the map," yet survived. Their kids were taken away to residential schools, and their languages and practices (like the potlatch) were often banned. We're now in a "recontact era." New relations are being negotiated based on mutual respect. Tymchak calls these "tectonic shifts" for Saskatchewan. It means changing the schools. But it also creates opportunities to "forge a new society," which is as much "theirs" as it is "ours," and can make us better as well as kinder.

He sees these shifts not just as a chance to do right by the downtrodden but for the whole society to become truer to itself. Public education was never public enough. It was too narrow and WASP-y, too "informed by Anglo-Christian values and deference to the ideals of British monarchy." Yet it contained the seeds of diversity and equity. Egerton Ryerson, the Methodist preacher who created Ontario's schools in the 19th century, might not recognize the results, or like them, but equity is what the system he launched was meant for. It's good for all kids, not just the neediest, to get a more complex, messier sense of the messy world they're part of. It's also more fun – and it's hard to learn if you're not having fun.

The late sociologist John Seeley told me that in the 1950s, he went from studying ghetto kids in Chicago to affluent families in Toronto's Forest Hill Village because he wanted to know if they were all deprived, in their ways. He said he found the well-off were probably even more troubled than the impoverished, because they sensed they were cut off from large chunks of reality by their privilege. Equity is a learning op for everyone. Its challenge is to expand the notion of public and transform the nature of education to correspond to it. Equity in the schools is really an answer to the question: Who are "we" now?

V. What is Public about Public Education?

Is there anything public schools do that no other form of education can? Only this: Simply by being what they are, they can teach kids about the society they live in. That's because public schools must let everyone in. What's unique about public education isn't the education part; it's the public. Other schools can tell kids about their society but they don't contain it and show it. At private school, kids can learn about the value of inclusiveness, but they're surrounded by others like themselves in key ways. In public schools the medium really is the message; the classroom is the curriculum. I don't mean to wear rose-coloured (or Rosedale-coloured) glasses. Every public school doesn't mirror our society perfectly. They're often residentially or socially segregated, so that rich kids go to school mainly with rich kids and poor with poor, etc. Still, others can slip in around the edges: Even in Toronto's affluent Rosedale area, there are kids who may rent on the fringes of those leafy streets, but they're at the same schools as a right.

Does this matter? Parents today tend to focus on schools giving their kids the skills, attitudes or credentials needed to survive in a scary work world. That's understandable. But there's no clear difference between public and private schools when it comes to providing this kind of preparation for the work world. Nor is there a guarantee that any of it will lead to a job in the fickle global marketplace.

Kids tend to have a different agenda than their parents. It's social. It has to do with other kids: getting to know them, learning to deal with them. It seems to me that their agenda probably makes more practical sense in the world as it now is than the parent agenda. In harsh, unpredictable times, a knack for things like community and democracy can be crucial. If so, public schools are uniquely equipped to handle that challenge. I'm thinking particularly about the ways that public schools can nurture the values of community and democracy.

A sense of community has always helped people through dark times. It's amazing how much economic stress they can withstand if they feel bound to others. Neighbourhood schools provide that kind of resource. But there are also forces working to undermine their community-building role.

Take school security. It seems like a no-brainer if there are safety risks. Lock the doors to keep out strangers, drug dealers etc. Mount security cameras. Hold lockdown drills. But however well-intentioned, these tend to teach paranoia at the expense of the alternative: learning what a community is. Few things build community as much as walking your kids to and from school in the early years and meeting others – and not just other parents – on the way or in the schoolyard or outside the classroom. If parents and local people can't come and go freely, you can lose the sense of connection to those living or working around the school.

Connection to the community that you're part of provides a different kind of security than you get by fencing off an enclave living in fear. The kids sense it. Those who gain a feel for community will become adults with an ear for it; those who don't, won't. These aren't easy issues to sort through, and good principals tend to agonize over how far to go, because they want kids to be safe but also know the value of a sense of community. Bad principals just slather on the security and let community wither.

Or take parents who protest the closing of a local school. They aren't always acting in narrow self-interest against school boards working within tight budgets. They may also be defending their communities.

I'm not being nostalgic. I know community is harder to find than it once was. That makes it even more important to nurture the sources that remain while working to cultivate new types. I happened to be at Toronto's George Webster Public School on Remembrance Day. It's a "model" school in a high needs area. Principal Nancy Steinhauer came from the "independent" sector, i.e., private schools. She says diplomatically that while there, "I always had a problem with the fact that not everyone was welcome."

Steve, the head custodian, coaches the hockey team, with players from Bangla Desh, Pakistan, and elsewhere. He says his own parents were Macedonian immigrants and didn't know from hockey, but a friend's mom asked if they could take him to play. It made him a Canadian. Now he's passing the torch to future generations. Steinhauer finagled ice-time and got equipment donated, which should be part of the principals' course, if it isn't. They observe Gandhi Day, Dia del Raza, International Women's Day, you name it. The parenting drop-in centre is open to all; you don't need to have a kid in the school.

For the Remembrance assembly, students in hijabs and teachers in saris recited "In Flanders Fields" and sang, "Where Have all the Flowers Gone?" Thus does a sense of community expand to include national history. A bemedaled vet of the Korean War spoke with brevity and dignity. The kids will build all that, along with hockey, into their notion of Canadian, which is what they're becoming. They're cobbling together an innovative sense of community.

With luck, whole new versions of it will emerge, and public schools are helping birth them. Principal Steinhauer at George Webster is the daughter of someone who taught me when I was a kid at my synagogue school – and my kid was taught at Clinton School by someone I taught in the same synagogue, when I was 16. It makes me feel a sense of garbled continuity in my own life, which is as much continuity as we often get to work with in this era.

Community in the past involved clearer links: geographic, ethnic, religious. Those versions are gone, probably forever. They had a claustrophobic downside along with the strong sense of belonging they provided. They were like one-room country schools, which are easy to romanticize but could also be stifling. Community remains a crucial need, maybe more so than ever with the disconnection and insecurity spread by globalization.

It's odd how often I found people teaching at schools they went to as kids; maybe it reflects that ancient need for clear connections. But for most of us now, a sense of community will have to be cobbled together using whatever fragments we can find: in real space, cyberspace, anywhere. It's futile to expect the sort of wholeness that existed (we imagine) in other ages. I know a kid whose friends decided to go to a small, intimate alternative school; he chose instead a big mainstream school. He liked it for its size, range of resources and sheer human variety. He was opting for a new kind of community over the old.

Democracy is something else that would be nice when you feel at the mercy of distant, impersonal forces. You can think of it as the right to speak your mind on public issues and wield a bit of power as well. That's what democratic politics is supposed to provide. But elections don't help much; you get to vote every few years and go home. Local school boards were once more accessible and real. Some actual citizen politics happened there. But they've been generally neutered by centralization. And parent councils mostly fundraise.

So it's another case where people have to cobble together a new version of the old: in this case, democratic involvement in the education system.

People for Education is a grassroots group begun by a group of moms who watched in horror what Mike Harris's provincial government was doing to their kids' schools during the late 1990s. They met for years around Annie Kidder's kitchen table in downtown Toronto, even after they became an influential province-wide group. Now they have an annual budget of $600,000. They figured out the politics and found their own way in. They were somehow naturally media savvy. They spent what they'd describe as a godawful amount of time devising gimmicks to draw enough media attention to make the points they wanted to raise. Then they'd rush home and make their kids' lunches or Hallowe'en costumes.

To gain political cred, and out of curiosity, they began collecting data on public schools that, amazingly, no one else had, including the Ministry of Education. The Ministry wound up going to them for info and treating them as a serious player. Annie Kidder says they still argue everything out "the way women do – very emotional, lots of touching each other." But once it's settled, they can be "pretty fascistic" about staying on message. It goes with their political smarts.

I suspect Mike Harris feels his life would have been perfect if it hadn't been for them. Their name used to sound wussy to me. But it's as sophisticated as the rest of their operation. It implies that everyone, not just parents or pros, has the right to meddle in public education. Kidder says it annoys her when parents say cutely, education is too important to be left to educators. She thinks it's too important to be left to any one group. The best hope is maximum democratic involvement because all of society has a stake in securing its future through the public schools.

This kind of activism is heartening, since there are strong non-democratic forces vying to control public education. The main influence in the U.S. now is big corporate money, coming through foundations like those started and financed by Bill Gates or Sam Walton. With fairly small sums, they've largely taken over the agenda by promoting private schools paid with public funds (charter schools) and seeding their own people in the public systems or insisting that administrators they favour remain in charge. Sometimes it's done with fairly small sums. A few hundred thousand dollars can buy a lot of compliance in a hard-pressed school district. They financed the richly-hyped documentary, "Waiting for Superman," which promotes charters and demonizes teachers' unions; and they partner with media like NBC to frame the debate as they see it.

I'm not accusing them of evil motives. The problem isn't that they view things in terms of their own business perspective and want to slap it all over the schools. The problem is they're unaccountable to anyone; but they have the money to take charge, much as corporations have taken over elections through campaign donations. So far their main thrust – charters, standardized tests, data-based accountability – has failed spectacularly, but serious damage is being done to a damaged system.

Speaking of unions, they take a pasting in the U.S. but, in most good public systems, they act as partners. Former B.C. Deputy Minister Charles Ungerleider says:

> With some exceptions, virtually every improvement in public education has been due to teacher bargaining rather than the government sector.

He has in mind services for kids with special needs, ESL programs, primary class size reductions, ratios for teacher-librarians according to school size, prep time (acknowledging that teachers don't work only while in class), professional development days, setting up teams to discuss progress of individual kids, mentorship programs and – going back a long way – job protection for women teachers when they marry and have kids. Unions mess up, and many parents wish it were easier to get rid of a bad teacher. But they operate in a fundamentally democratic way and are a potential democratic resource.

Can democracy extend right into classrooms? That does sound odd. But kids learn more from what they see than from what they're formally taught. If a school proclaims, "This month's value is respect" – which happens in Ontario – the kids will check it against how their teachers treat students. Kids are always checking stuff that comes from adults. Learning about democracy doesn't mean knowing the levels of government and your obligation to vote. It starts with how seriously your right to have your own thoughts and opinions is treated.

This is where teaching comes in. If a school focuses on marks, and teaches to the test, kids will concentrate on reproducing correct answers, not on developing their ability to think. They'll see each other as competition rather than learning to solve problems together, which is how most issues get handled in the real world. Even in a personal crisis, you seek help from others who know you. This is especially true for thinking in a democracy, where common (as in: everyone has it) sense is the way to reach decisions. Learning mainly to take tests and replicate answers produces stupid people who can't think much for themselves. This might help explain the dismal level of debate in U.S. elections. They do the best they can in the light of the tools they weren't given.

So what you're taught matters less than how you're taught. A curriculum can be good, bad, or even offensive. As long as teachers encourage you to think about it, you'll soon learn to think for yourself and engage with others. Of course you can learn to think, and think democratically, in a private school. But the public system ought to be democratic thinking's natural home.

Is this kind of mental democratic training useful, at a time when people worry most about the loss of good jobs? I'd say it's totally useful. No private person facing a bad economy can do much about the choices before them. As individuals, they have to pick up whatever scraps (or jobs) are tossed their way. But people working together have often changed the shape of their society – in health care, jobs, many areas – by thinking, arguing, agreeing, then acting.

Jobs aren't the only crisis; there's the environment. Kids are natural environmental idealists, but they need the tools to devise a plan, once they realize that their dismay alone won't change things. It requires everyone to pitch in, and the public schools include everyone. They're the natural place to rally the forces.

This also means there's no one right way to prepare kids for the future they face. Democratically speaking, that would be undemocratic. In a way, democracy is education: everyone learning from everyone else. One thing I've discovered in exploring this subject is there's no deep mystery of education with a universal solution waiting to be revealed. Anyone who says they have it – and many do – is probably trying to build a career or sell a product. Lots of things work. Almost anything can, and it can also stop working, if you ease up.

I've always felt involved in education myself. I've taught, though only part time, since my teens. I often wrote about education, and if asked what right I had to do so, since I had no kids, I'd mutter, "Well, I was a kid." But my early interest centered on personal liberation through "free schools" or self-discovery. Then, 12 years ago, I became a dad. For kindergarten, my kid went to a private Montessori school; and in Grade 1, into the public system. I was nervous about the move but he wasn't. You could see a sort of six-year-old swagger in him as he walked the halls of our local school. As if he knew it was part of the real world in a way the sheltered fishbowl of Montessori wasn't. And I was amazed at the sense of community I felt standing around with others in the schoolyard. Toronto has to be as great a place to find your own route in public education as there could be. Kids I know sense the privilege of being in school here, less due to the formal teaching they get than to the hugely varied "public" they go into classes with.

Canadians have tended to define ourselves as a society in terms of public health care, and that is an achievement to take pride in. But public education is an accomplishment on a different level. Health care is biological; it's about survival on a physical level, and it's similar for people everywhere. Education is more specific and social. It's how we define the way we are, not simply that we are.